What Is a Globe?

Monday

1. A globe is a model of _____.

2. Is a globe bigger or smaller than Earth?

   _____

Tuesday

1. A globe is _____ like the Earth.

         round   flat

2. A globe shows land and _____.

Wednesday

1. A continent is a large area of _____.

2. Name one of the continents shown on the picture of the globe.

   _____

What Is a Globe?

Thursday

1. An ocean is a large body of _____.

2. Name one of the oceans shown on the picture of the globe.

   _____

Friday

1. What do the words on the globe tell you?

   _____

2. Does the Earth have more land or water?

   _____

Challenge

Color North America green. Color South America yellow. Color the oceans blue.

What Is a Map?

Monday

1. Is a map flat or round?

   _____

2. What does this map show?

          all of Earth   part of Earth

Tuesday

1. Circle the things you see on this map.

        animals   land   people   water

2. The directions on the map are north, _____, east,

   and _____ .

Wednesday

1. The map shows two continents. What are their names?

   _____

   _____

2. Are continents the largest or smallest land areas on Earth?

   _____

What Is a Map?

Thursday

1. Which ocean is in the north?

_____

2. Which ocean is in the west?

_____

Friday

1. Which continent looks bigger in size?

_____

2. Is the United States in North America or South America?

_____

Challenge

Color North America green. Color South America yellow. Color the oceans blue. If you live in North America, make a red X on it.

Directions on a Map

Monday

1. What does the map show?

   a park   a farm   a school

2. What is the name of the park?

   _____

Tuesday

1. A compass rose shows _____ .

   directions   people   places

2. Name the four directions on the compass rose.

   _____   _____

   _____   _____

Wednesday

1. Is the baseball diamond in the north or south?

   _____

2. Which area of the park is in the south?

   _____

Directions on a Map

Thursday

1. The swimming pool is in the _____ .

   east   west

2. The picnic area is in the _____ .

   east   west

Friday

1. The baseball diamond is _____ of the entrance.

   east   west

2. The swimming pool is north of the _____ .

   baseball diamond   playground

Challenge

Look at the compass rose. Color the arrow pointing north red.
Color the arrow pointing south blue. Color the arrow pointing east
yellow. Color the arrow pointing west green.

Using Directions

Monday

1. The map shows a _____ .

   city   park   school

2. Circle the places where games are played.

   baseball diamond   cafeteria   parking lot   soccer field

Tuesday

1. The _____ shows four directions.

2. Which direction does "N" stand for?

   _____

Wednesday

1. On the compass rose, which direction is pointing down?

   _____

2. Which directions do "E" and "W" stand for?

   _____

Using Directions

Thursday

1. Find the baseball diamond. It is _____ of the cafeteria.

   north   south

2. The soccer field is _____ of the baseball diamond.

   east   west

Friday

1. The playground is _____ of the parking lot.

2. What is closest to the school building?

   baseball diamond   playground   parking lot

Challenge

Do you think the playground is in a good location? Write about where you think the playground should be. Write your answer on the back of the map.

A Map Key

Monday

1. What does the map show?

   a park   a school   a playground

2. What does the map key show?

   directions   symbols   title

Tuesday

1. Which is the symbol for a campground?

2. What does the symbol ⌒ stand for?

   _____

Wednesday

1. What does the symbol stand for?

   _____

2. What does the bridge go over?

   _____

A Map Key

Thursday

1. Where is the girl fishing?

   _____

2. How many picnic areas are on the map? _____

Friday

1. Which is closest to the campground?

   lake   picnic area   trail

2. What is at the end of the trail?

   hills   lake   woods

Challenge

What other things are found at a nature park? Choose one more thing to add to the park map. Draw a symbol for it on the map key. Then draw it on the map.

Using a Map Key

WEEK 6

Monday

1. The map shows a _____.

     large city   neighborhood   state

2. Name two things shown on the map.

_____

_____

Tuesday

1. How many symbols are on the map key? _____

2. Which is a symbol for the park?

Wednesday

1. How many houses are in the neighborhood?

_____

2. What is across the street from the park?

     gas station   library   school

Using a Map Key

Thursday

1. What is east of the library?

   _____

2. What is <u>not</u> on the map?

   gas station   library   police station

Friday

1. The gas station is between Bell Avenue and _____ Avenue.

2. The bus stop is at the corner of which two streets?

   _____

   _____

Challenge

Color each symbol on the map key a different color. Then color the pictures on the map to match. For example, color the school symbol red. On the map, color the school red.

A Map Grid

Monday

1. The map shows a _____.

   playground   park   zoo

2. A grid is shown on the map. The grid lines make _____.

   circles   squares   triangles

Tuesday

1. The zoo map is in a grid. Which letters are on the grid map?

   _____

2. Which numbers are on the grid map?

   _____

Wednesday

1. Which animals are in grid square A2?

   _____

2. Which animals are in grid square B4?

   _____

A Map Grid

Thursday

1. In which grid squares are these animals?

    lions _____

    tigers _____

    bears _____

2. What kind of animals are in the aviary?

    _____

Friday

1. What kind of animals are in the reptile house?

    _____

2. Start at the entrance. Which grid squares would you go through
    to see the hippos?

    _____

Challenge

Color the areas on the map where you can eat and rest.

Using a Map Grid

Monday

1. The map shows the state of _____ .

2. How many cities are shown on the map? _____

Tuesday

1. The map is in a grid. What is a grid?

    _____

    _____

    _____

2. Which letters and numbers are shown on the grid?

    _____

Wednesday

1. Which city is in the B1 square?

    _____

2. Which two cities are near Lake Erie?

    _____

Using a Map Grid

Thursday

1. Which cities are in the letter B squares?

   _____

2. Which cities are in the number 2 squares?

   _____

Friday

1. What is the capital of Ohio? In which grid square is it found?

   _____

2. Which cities are near the Ohio River? In which squares are they found?

   _____

   _____

Challenge

On the map, trace the Ohio River in blue. On the back of the map, write the squares that the Ohio River runs through.

Picturing a Place

Monday

1. What does this map show?

   a bedroom   a classroom   a library

2. Where is the door?

   in the front   in the back   on the side

Tuesday

1. How many windows are there?

   _____

2. Circle all the places where there are windows.

   front   back   right   left

Wednesday

1. The student desks face the _____ of the classroom.

   front   back

2. The computers are at the _____ of the classroom.

   front   back

Picturing a Place

Thursday

1. Name two things at the front of the classroom.

   _____

2. Name two things at the back of the classroom.

   _____

Friday

1. What is on the right side of the table?

   _____

2. If you are sitting at a computer, where is the teacher's desk?

   behind you   in front of you   to the left of you

Challenge

Look at the map for one minute. Turn the map over so you can't see it. Close your eyes. Think about the classroom. Now open your eyes. Draw one thing from the classroom.

Picturing the United States

Monday

1. The title of the map is _____.

   Our Country   Picturing the United States

2. The map shows _____ of the United States.

   all   part

Tuesday

1. The United States is a _____ country.

   large   small

2. The map shows _____ .

   48 states   50 states

Wednesday

1. Which state is in the north?

   North Dakota   Texas

2. Which state is in the south?

   Minnesota   Louisiana

Picturing the United States

Thursday

1. Which state is in the east?

   Nevada   Virginia

2. Which state is in the west?

   California   North Carolina

Friday

1. Which state is larger in size?

   Alaska   Hawaii

2. Which part of the U.S. has larger states in size?

   the east part   the west part

Challenge

What is the name of your state?

_____

Color your state on the map.

A Street Map of Parker

Monday

1. The map shows the town of _____.

2. Name two places in Parker.

   _____

Tuesday

1. How many streets and avenues are in Parker?

   _____

2. In which directions does Main Street go?

   north and south   east and west

Wednesday

1. Name the things you see on Fourth Avenue.

   _____

   _____

2. What is across Main Street from the school?

   park   post office   youth center

A Street Map of Parker

Thursday

1. Which is the most important street in Parker?

   _____

2. Which street has the most buildings on it?

   _____

Friday

1. What is the route from the park to the youth center?

   _____

   _____

2. Which building is the farthest away from Joe's house?

   post office   school

Challenge

Joe rides his bike to school. What is Joe's route from home to school? Draw a line from Joe's house to the school. Then write the streets he followed on the map.

Daily Geography Practice • EMC 6852 • © Evan-Moor Corp.

A Road Map of Nebraska

Monday

1. The map shows cities and _____.

   highways   bike paths   streets

2. The map shows the state of _____.

   Iowa   Nebraska   South Dakota

Tuesday

1. Which interstate highway runs across Nebraska?

   _____

2. Which U.S. highways are shown on the map?

   _____

Wednesday

1. What is the capital of Nebraska?

   _____

2. The capital is on which highway?

   _____

A Road Map of Nebraska

Thursday

1. Which city on Interstate 80 is closer to Lincoln?

    Omaha   Kearney

2. Which highway runs north and south?

    _____

Friday

1. Which city on U.S. Highway 20 is west of Valentine?

    Bassett   Chadron

2. Which city is found where Interstate 80 and U.S. Highway 83 meet?

    _____

Challenge

Follow the route from Valentine to Lincoln. Write the route you would take to travel from Valentine to Lincoln on the map.

Daily Geography Practice • EMC 6852 • © Evan-Moor Corp.

A World Map

Monday

1. The map shows the whole _____.

2. The map shows large areas of land and _____.

Tuesday

1. The large land areas are called _____.

    continents   oceans

2. There are _____ continents of the world.

Wednesday

1. Name the five oceans of the world.

    _____

    _____

    _____

    _____

    _____

2. Which ocean is the farthest north in the world?

    _____

A World Map

Thursday

1. Four continents border the Atlantic Ocean. Name two of them.

_____

2. Four continents border the Pacific Ocean. Name two of them.

_____

Friday

1. Asia is the largest continent. Which continent is the smallest in size?

_____

2. Which continent is the coldest and farthest south?

_____

Challenge

Color the continents green. Color the oceans blue. Put a red X on the continent you live on.

A Land and Water Map of Washington

Monday

1. The map shows the state of _____ .

2. Washington has many forests and _____ .

   deserts   mountains

Tuesday

1. The Olympic Mountains and the _____ Mountains are in Washington.

2. Washington is called the "Evergreen State" because it has many _____ .

   lakes   forests

Wednesday

1. Name the highest mountain in Washington.

   _____

2. Which volcano erupted in 1980?

   _____

A Land and Water Map of Washington

WEEK 14

Thursday

1. Which river is the longest in Washington?

   _____

2. Which two rivers join the Columbia River?

   _____

Friday

1. Puget Sound is a long _____ .

   area of land   body of water

2. Which two cities border Puget Sound?

   _____

Challenge

Draw and color a picture of a volcano. Write **Mount Saint Helens** at the top of the page. Write the definition of a volcano under the picture. Attach your picture to the map.

28   Daily Geography Practice • EMC 6852 • © Evan-Moor Corp.

A Land and Water Map of Arizona

Monday

1. The map shows the state of _____.

2. Arizona has canyons, _____,

   and _____.

Tuesday

1. Which two rivers are on the map?

   _____

2. What is the capital of Arizona?

   _____

Wednesday

1. Which desert is located in northern Arizona?

   _____

2. Which desert is near Tucson?

   _____

A Land and Water Map of Arizona

Thursday

1. _____ is a famous canyon in Arizona.

2. Which river flows through the Grand Canyon?

   _____

Friday

1. The Grand Canyon is made up of _____ .

   layers of colorful rocks

   layers of brown mud

   layers of white sand

2. What colors can be found on the canyon walls?

   _____

   _____

Challenge

On the map, color the Grand Canyon red, yellow, brown, and green. Color the rivers blue. Color the deserts yellow. Color the mountains brown.

A Land and Water Map of Hawaii

Monday

1. The map shows the state of _____ .

   Arizona   California   Hawaii

2. Hawaii has _____ main islands.

Tuesday

1. Hawaii is located in the _____ Ocean.

2. The largest island in the state is called _____ .

   Hawaii   Maui   Oahu

Wednesday

1. What is the capital of Hawaii?

   _____

   On which island is it located?

   _____

2. Hawaii is located _____ of the rest of the United States.

   south and west   north and east

A Land and Water Map of Hawaii

Thursday

1. Which island has Kilauea Volcano on it?

   _____

2. An island and a volcano are called landforms. What other landform is shown on some of the islands?

   desert   forest   mountain

Friday

1. What does it mean when a volcano is active?

   It is sleeping.

   It sends out lava, gases, and ashes.

   It won't erupt ever again.

2. The Haleakala Crater is a volcano that is not active. On which island is it?

   _____

Challenge

Color each island a different color. Color the Pacific Ocean blue.

A Land and Water Map of Florida

Monday

1. The map shows the state of _____.

2. Florida is in the shape of _____.

   an island   a mountain   a peninsula

Tuesday

1. Which ocean is east of Florida?

   Atlantic Ocean   Arctic Ocean   Pacific Ocean

2. Which gulf is west of Florida?

_____

Wednesday

1. What is the capital of Florida?

_____

2. Name the city farthest south in Florida on the map.

_____

A Land and Water Map of Florida

Thursday

1. Which group of islands is part of Florida?

   _____

2. The states of Georgia and _____ border Florida.

Friday

1. Which bay has the same name as a city?

   _____

2. Is a bay or a gulf larger in size?

   _____

Challenge

Color the state of Florida yellow. Remember to color the islands called the Florida Keys. Color all the water blue. Remember to color Lake Okeechobee.

A Land and Water Map of Minnesota

Monday

1. The map shows the state of _____ .

2. Minnesota is famous for its _____ .

   lakes   oceans   ponds

Tuesday

1. What is the capital of Minnesota?

   _____

2. Red Lake is very big and has two parts. What are they called?

   _____

Wednesday

1. Where does the Mississippi River begin?

   Lake Itasca   Lower Red Lake   Mille Lacs Lake

2. Which city is <u>not</u> near the Mississippi River?

   Bemidji   Duluth   Minneapolis

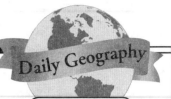

A Land and Water Map of Minnesota

Thursday

1. The largest lake in the U.S. borders Minnesota. What is its name?

   _____

2. Which lake is between the Mississippi and the St. Croix Rivers?

   _____

Friday

1. Minnesota borders the country of _____.

2. Which lake shares a border with Minnesota and Canada?

   _____

Challenge

On the map, color the rivers dark blue. Color all the lakes a light blue.

A Rural Area Map

Monday

1. The map shows two _____ .

    cities   farms   towns

2. Name two animals shown on the farms.

    _____

    _____

Tuesday

1. The people on the farm live in the _____ .

    house   barn

2. The animals on the farm live in the _____ .

    house   barn

Wednesday

1. Name the road between the two farms.

    _____

2. Circle the kinds of transportation shown on the map.

    airplane   bus   car   tractor   truck   van

A Rural Area Map

Thursday

1. What is north and east of the rural area?

   _____

2. Which two roads do farmers follow to town?

   _____

Friday

1. A rural area has _____ .

   farms and countryside

   large cities

   states and countries

2. Which area has more people?

   a city   a farming community   the countryside

Challenge

Where would you like to live? Would it be a rural area or a big city? Why? Write your answer on the map.

Daily Geography Practice • EMC 6852 • © Evan-Moor Corp.

A Suburb Map

Monday

1. The map shows mostly a _____ .

   city   farm   suburb

2. Is the suburb close to a city or a farming area?

   _____

Tuesday

1. What is the name of the suburb?

   _____

2. Which big city is Elgin close to?

   _____

Wednesday

1. The suburb has stores and _____ .

2. The stores are on which street in Elgin?

   _____

A Suburb Map

Thursday

1. Which major road goes from the suburb toward the city?

   _____

2. Which streets cross Villa Street?

   _____

Friday

1. More houses and stores are _____ of Villa Street.

         east   west

2. What is a suburb?

   _____

Challenge

Would you rather live in a city or in a suburb? Why? Write your answer on the map.

A City Map

Monday

1. The map shows a _____.

   city   rural area   suburb

2. The buildings in the city are _____.

   close together   far apart

Tuesday

1. The city map does <u>not</u> show _____.

   highways   sidewalks   streets

2. Which building is a home for people?

   an apartment   a bank   a museum

Wednesday

1. Which building in the city saves people's money for them?

   a bank   a museum   a store

2. Which of these is next to the apartments?

   a museum   a park   a store

A City Map

Thursday

1. Special things about science are found at the _____.

   bank   department store   museum

2. Why are people looking into the store window?

   _____

Friday

1. The city has very tall buildings. What is another name for a tall building in a city?

   apartment   bank   skyscraper

2. A city is a busy and crowded place. What does **crowded** mean?

   There are lots of people.

   There are some people.

   There are a few people.

Challenge

What would you name the city on the map? Write the name on the map.

A State Map

Monday

1. The map shows the state of _____ .

   California   Georgia   Texas

2. Name two cities in Georgia.

   _____

Tuesday

1. Which symbol stands for the capital?

2. What is the capital of Georgia?

   _____

Wednesday

1. How many states border or touch Georgia?

   _____

2. Which state borders Georgia to the south?

   _____

A State Map

Thursday

1. The Chattahoochee River is a border for Georgia and _____.

   Alabama   South Carolina   Tennessee

2. Which river borders Georgia and South Carolina?

   _____

Friday

1. Which large body of water borders Georgia?

   _____

2. Where is Georgia located in the United States?

   Northeast   Southeast

Challenge

Follow the border lines of Georgia with your finger. Then draw a dark line around the state of Georgia.

An Amusement Park

Monday

1. The map shows _____ park.

   an amusement   a city   a nature

2. How many rides are at the amusement park? _____

Tuesday

1. Name three rides you can go on at the amusement park.

   _____

   _____

   _____

2. Where is the food and picnic area in the park?

   at the entrance   in the middle   near the exit

Wednesday

1. Which ride gets you all wet?

   _____

2. The clown is standing by which ride?

   _____

An Amusement Park

Thursday

1. Which two rides are safer for little children?

   _____

2. Which ride is very fast and goes up and down?

   _____

Friday

1. What two things are near the entrance?

   _____

   _____

2. Are the restrooms closer to the entrance or to the exit?

   _____

Challenge

You get to name the amusement park. What would you call it?
Write the name of the park on the map. Now color your new
amusement park in bright colors.

Mount Rushmore

Monday

1. The map shows the state of _____.

   Minnesota   North Dakota   South Dakota

2. _____ is a huge stone memorial of four presidents.

   Mount Rushmore

   The Statue of Liberty

   The White House

Tuesday

1. How many presidents are on Mount Rushmore? _____

2. Thomas Jefferson, Abraham Lincoln, Theodore Roosevelt, and

   _____ are on Mount Rushmore.

Wednesday

1. Mount Rushmore is located in the _____ of South Dakota.

   Black Hills   Redwood Forest   Rocky Mountains

2. Is Mount Rushmore east or west of the Missouri River?

   _____

Mount Rushmore

Thursday

1. Mount Rushmore is between which two cities?

   _____

2. What is the capital of South Dakota? _____

   Is it near Mount Rushmore? _____

Friday

1. Which city on Interstate 90 is farthest away from Mount Rushmore?

   _____

2. What two kinds of natural features are near Mount Rushmore?

   canyons   mountains   plains
   and deserts   and forests   and grasslands

Challenge

Draw a line from the president to something important he did. One of them has been done for you.

President	Honor
Thomas Jefferson	was first president of the U.S.
Abraham Lincoln	helped set up the national forests.
Theodore Roosevelt	ended slavery in the U.S.
George Washington	wrote the Declaration of Independence.

A Weather Map

Monday

1. What kind of map is shown?

   a land and water map   a road map   a weather map

2. How many states are shown on the large map?

   _____

Tuesday

1. What is the symbol for partly cloudy?

2. Which state is having a sunny day?

   _____

Wednesday

1. What kind of weather is Nebraska having?

   _____

2. People in South Dakota are having a _____ day.

   rainy   snowy   sunny

A Weather Map

Thursday

1. Which states are probably the coldest?

   _____

   _____

2. If it gets colder in South Dakota, what might happen to the weather?

   _____

Friday

1. The five states are located in the _____ part of the United States.

   eastern   northern   southern   western

2. Probably which month and season is it for the five states?

   August, summer   May, spring

   January, winter   September, fall

Challenge

Which state has your favorite kind of weather? Write the name of the state on the map. Write why you like that kind of weather.

A Desert Habitat

Monday

1. The map shows _____ .

   a desert   a forest   grasslands

2. A home for animals and plants is called their _____ .

Tuesday

1. Name two animals shown on the desert map.

   _____

2. Name two plants shown on the desert map.

   _____

   _____

Wednesday

1. What is the air mostly like on the desert?

   cold and rainy   hot and dry   warm and wet

2. What is the land mostly like on the desert?

   grass and hills   moss and woods   rocks and sand

A Desert Habitat

Thursday

1. Deserts get less than _____ of rain each year.

   1 inch   5 inches   10 inches

2. How do many animals hunt for food in the hot desert?

   They hunt for food during the day when it's hotter.

   They hunt for food during the night when it's cooler.

Friday

1. Some people's houses are made from clay bricks called

   _____.

2. Adobe houses help keep people _____ in the desert.

   cool   hot   warm

Challenge

Look at the list of animals on the map. Choose your favorite. Find out what it looks like. Draw the animal on the map.

A Population Map of California

Monday

1. The map shows the state of _____ .

2. The map shows the _____ largest cities and

   _____ capital.

Tuesday

1. What is the capital of California?

   _____

2. Which California city has the largest population?

   _____

Wednesday

1. Which city is the second largest in population?

   _____

2. Which two cities are 3rd and 4th in population?

   _____

   _____

A Population Map of California

Thursday

1. Which of the five largest cities is not on the coast?

   _____

2. What is the same about all the cities?

   Their names start with the letter "S."

   They are located in the southern part of California.

   They are the largest cities in California.

Friday

1. California has the _____ population in the United States.

   largest   smallest

2. California has over _____ million people.

Challenge

The population is counted every 10 years. The last time people were counted was in the year 2010. When will people be counted again? Solve this math problem in the box.

┌───┐
│   │
│   │
│   │
│   │
└───┘

A County Fair Map

Monday

1. The map shows a _____ .

   barn with animals   county fair   playground

2. There are five areas on the map. Name two of them.

   _____

Tuesday

1. Name three animals at the county fair.

   _____

   _____

2. Name two kinds of food sold at the county fair.

   _____

Wednesday

1. Where do you go into the county fair?

   in the north   in the south

2. What things are shown in the arts and crafts area?

   _____

   _____

A County Fair Map

Thursday

1. Look at the carnival area. Name three things you see there.

   _____

   _____

   _____

2. There is a stage at the county fair. What is happening there?

   _____

   _____

Friday

1. Which areas are on either side of the entrance gate?

   _____

2. Which area is farthest from the entrance gate?

   animals   arts and crafts   carnival

Challenge

Color your favorite area at the county fair. Write a sentence telling why you like this area the best on the map.

A Product Map of Kansas

Monday

1. The map shows the state of _____.

2. The map shows _____.

   farm products   population   weather

Tuesday

1. Circle the symbol for hogs.

2. Circle the symbol for wheat.

Wednesday

1. Kansas grows more _____ than any other state.

   corn   sorghum   wheat

2. Name two animals that farmers raise in Kansas.

   _____

A Product Map of Kansas

Thursday

1. What are the top two farm products?

   _____

2. Which farm product is shown near the capital?

   corn   hogs   sorghum grain

Friday

1. Kansas is called "The Wheat State." Why?

   _____

   _____

2. Kansas is called "The Breadbasket of America." Why?

   _____

   _____

Challenge

What kinds of things are made from wheat? On the map, draw a product that is made from wheat.

Living in a Community

Monday

1. The map shows _____ in a community.

   homes   parks   stores

2. How many streets are there in the community? _____

Tuesday

1. Name one kind of home on the map.

   _____

2. The apartment buildings are on which street?

   _____

Wednesday

1. Which street has one-story houses on it?

   _____

2. Which street has two-story houses on it?

   _____

Living in a Community

Thursday

1. A duplex has two homes together. On which street can you find duplexes?

   _____

2. How many duplexes are on this map?

   _____

Friday

1. Which two streets do <u>not</u> have any driveways that open onto them?

   _____

2. Where is the mobile home park?

   _____

Challenge

What kind of home would you like to live in? Draw this home in the empty lot on the map page.

Community Services

Monday

1. The map shows _____ .

    community   parks and   shopping
    services   playground   malls

2. Name two community services on the map.

    _____

Tuesday

1. The _____ is a good place to mail a letter.

    library   post office   school

2. The _____ is a good place to go when you are sick.

    hospital   library   police station

Wednesday

1. Where could you go to ask for help?

    the fire   the police   both the fire station
    station   station   and police station

2. What is the job of community service workers?

    to have fun   to help people   to make money

Community Services

Thursday

1. When you hear a siren, you know there is _____ .

    an emergency   a parade   a party

2. Which is used in an emergency?

    an ambulance   a bus   a car

Friday

1. The hospital helps with an emergency. Which two other places help with emergencies?

    _____

2. If you want to find a book to read, where could you go?

    _____

Challenge

Which community helper would you like to be? Choose one from the list. Write why you would like to be that helper on the map.

    bus driver   doctor   firefighter   librarian

    mail carrier   nurse   teacher   police officer

Cattle Ranches in Texas

Monday

1. The map shows the state of _____ .

   Alaska   California   Texas

2.  stands for _____ on the map.

Tuesday

1. How many cattle ranch areas are on the map?

   _____

2. Most of the cattle in Texas are _____ cattle.

   beef   dairy

Wednesday

1. Cattle ranches are in _____ of the state.

   a small part   half   most parts

2. What is the capital of Texas? _____

   Are cattle ranches near the capital? _____

Cattle Ranches in Texas

Thursday

1. A large group of cattle is called a _____.

2. Texas is number _____ in the United States for beef cattle.

Friday

1. Which city does <u>not</u> have cattle ranches nearby?

    Amarillo   Brownsville   San Antonio

2. Cowboys and cowgirls ride _____ to round up beef cattle.

Challenge

Would you like to be a cowboy or cowgirl in Texas? Why or why not? Write your answer on the map.

A Tourist Map of Hawaii

Monday

1. The map shows the state of _____ .

   Alaska   California   Hawaii

2. There are _____ main islands in Hawaii.

Tuesday

1. The map is a _____ map of Hawaii.

   city   tourist   weather

2. Hawaii is located in the _____ Ocean.

   Atlantic   Indian   Pacific

Wednesday

1. What is the capital of Hawaii? _____

   Which island is it on? _____

2. Name two tourist places on the island of Oahu.

   _____

   _____

A Tourist Map of Hawaii

Thursday

1. What is the big island called **Hawaii** famous for?

   _____

2. Name three islands you could visit besides Oahu and Hawaii.

   _____

   _____

   _____

Friday

1. What is the title of the travel booklet?

   _____

2. Name two things the travel booklet tells you to do in Hawaii.

   _____

   _____

Challenge

Which island in Hawaii would you most like to visit? Why? Write your answer on the map. Color your favorite island in Hawaii, too.

A Resource Map of Maine

Monday

1. The map shows the state of _____ .

   Maine   Michigan   Minnesota

2. The map shows Maine's _____ .

   farm products   population   natural resources

Tuesday

1. 🌲 is a symbol for a _____ .

2. 🦞 is a symbol for a _____ .

Wednesday

1. Name two natural resources of Maine.

   _____

   _____

2. Which ocean is east of Maine?

   _____

A Resource Map of Maine

Thursday

1. What is the capital of Maine? _____

   Which river is it near? _____

2. The mountains are in the _____ part of the state.

   western   eastern

Friday

1. What is Maine's state animal?

   _____

2. Maine is called "The Pine Tree State." Why?

   _____

   _____

Challenge

On the map, color the forests green. Color the water blue. Color the animals, too.

Clarksville: Then and Now

Monday

1. The map shows the town of _____.

2. The map shows Clarksville 150 years ago and _____.

   today   tomorrow

Tuesday

1. The top map is a _____ map of Clarksville.

   history   product   weather

2. The top map shows Clarksville _____ years ago.

Wednesday

1. Clarksville 150 years ago was a _____.

   big city   farming community   suburb

2. Clarksville today is a _____.

   farming community   town   neighborhood

Clarksville: Then and Now

Thursday

1. How have the buildings changed in 150 years?

     Many buildings are larger and taller now.

     Many buildings are smaller now.

     The buildings now have windows.

2. Name one thing that has <u>not</u> changed about Clarksville.

   _____

Friday

1. Name a modern invention you see in Clarksville today.

   _____

2. How has transportation changed in Clarksville?

   _____

   _____

Challenge

Do you like Clarksville better then or now? Why? Write your answer on the map.

A Neighborhood Plan

Monday

1. The map shows a _____.

   nature park   neighborhood   state

2. The neighborhood has four _____.

   schools   houses   streets

Tuesday

1. Name the streets in the neighborhood.

   _____

   _____

2. Which street is the longest one in the neighborhood?

   _____

Wednesday

1. Where can people go to get gas and a snack?

   _____

2. On Rose Avenue, there is a _____ and houses.

A Neighborhood Plan

Thursday

1. What is south of the Quick Stop?

   _____

2. What is south of Lily Lane?

   _____

Friday

1. Which area is the smallest?

   a city   a neighborhood   a state

2. Which area in the neighborhood is probably <u>not</u> taken care of?

   empty lot   Garden Elementary   Quick Stop

Challenge

Look at the map. What would you build in the empty lot? Draw it in the empty lot.

What Is a Globe?

A globe is a model of the Earth. It is round like the Earth.

A globe shows the continents. Continents are the large areas of land.

A globe shows oceans. Oceans are large
bodies of salt water.

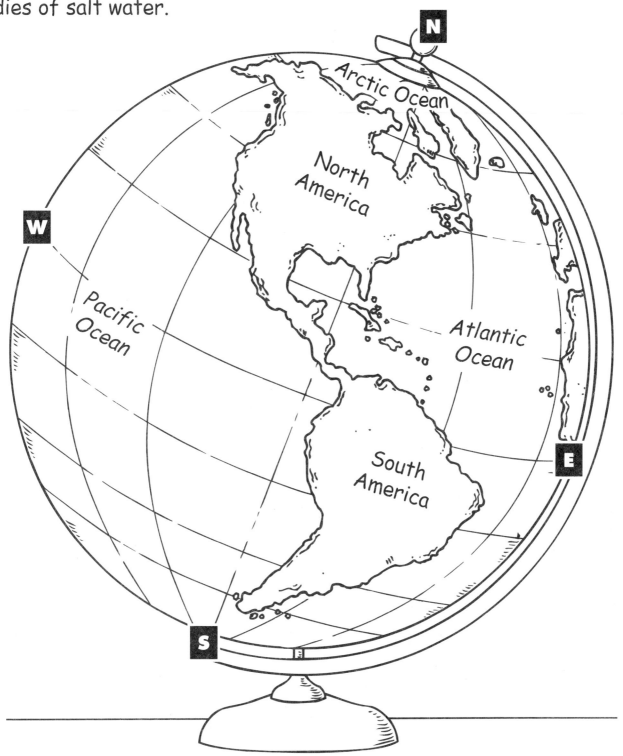

What Is a Map?

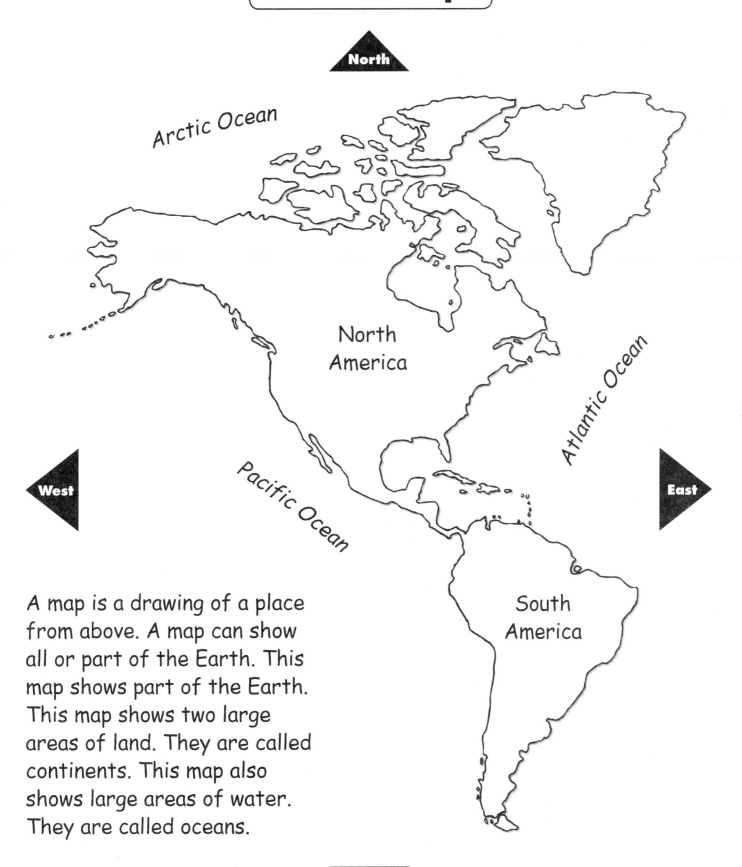

A map is a drawing of a place from above. A map can show all or part of the Earth. This map shows part of the Earth. This map shows two large areas of land. They are called continents. This map also shows large areas of water. They are called oceans.

Daily Geography Practice • EMC 6852 • © Evan-Moor Corp.

Directions on a Map

Using Directions

Soccer Field

Baseball Diamond

Playground

Cafeteria

Parking Lot/Buses

Nelson Elementary

NELSON ELEMENTARY

A Map Key

Using a Map Key

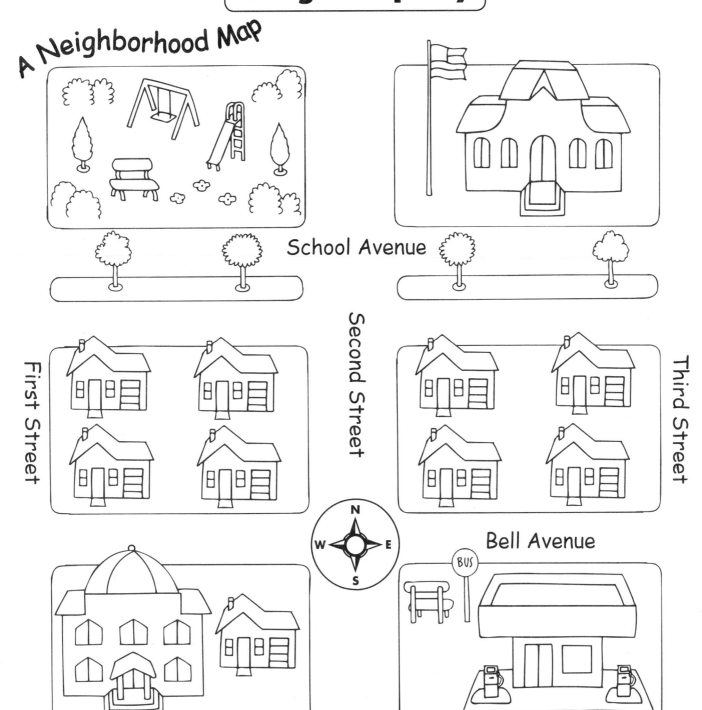

A Neighborhood Map

School Avenue

Second Street

First Street

Third Street

Bell Avenue

Busy Avenue

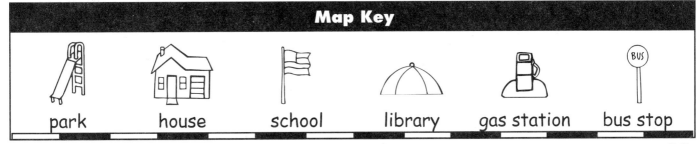

Map Key

park   house   school   library   gas station   bus stop

A Map Grid

This map is in a grid. A grid is a pattern of lines. The lines form squares. A grid helps you find places on the map.

Using a Map Grid

This map shows some cities in Ohio. The map is in a grid. A grid is a pattern of lines. The lines form small squares.

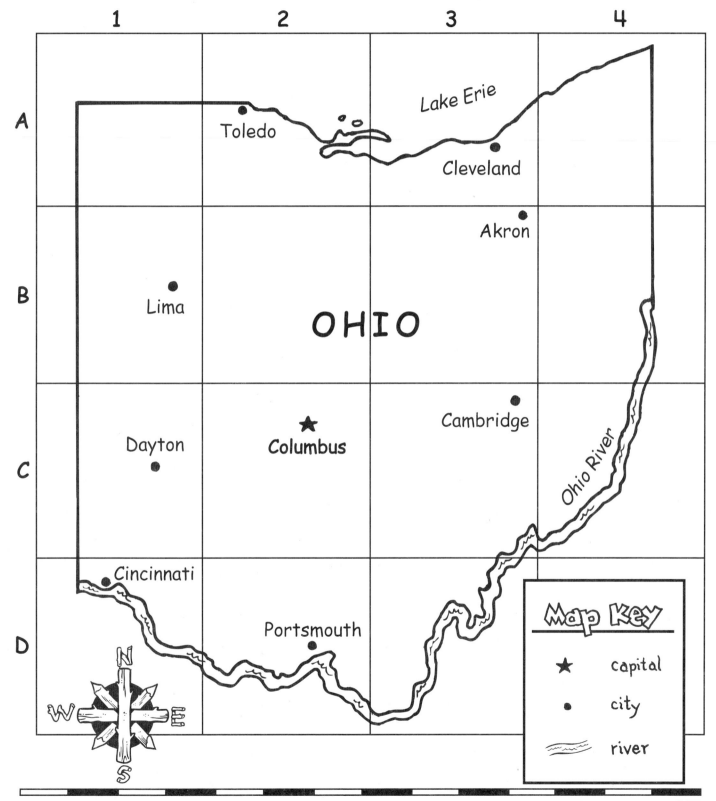

Picturing a Place

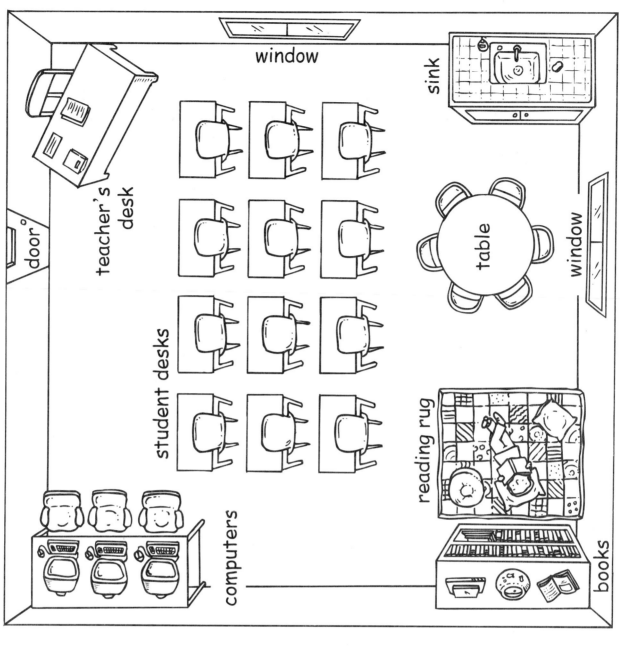

Classroom Map

This is a map of a classroom.

Look at it for one minute.

Then close your eyes.

Think about what is in the classroom.

Open your eyes.

Were you right?

Picturing the United States

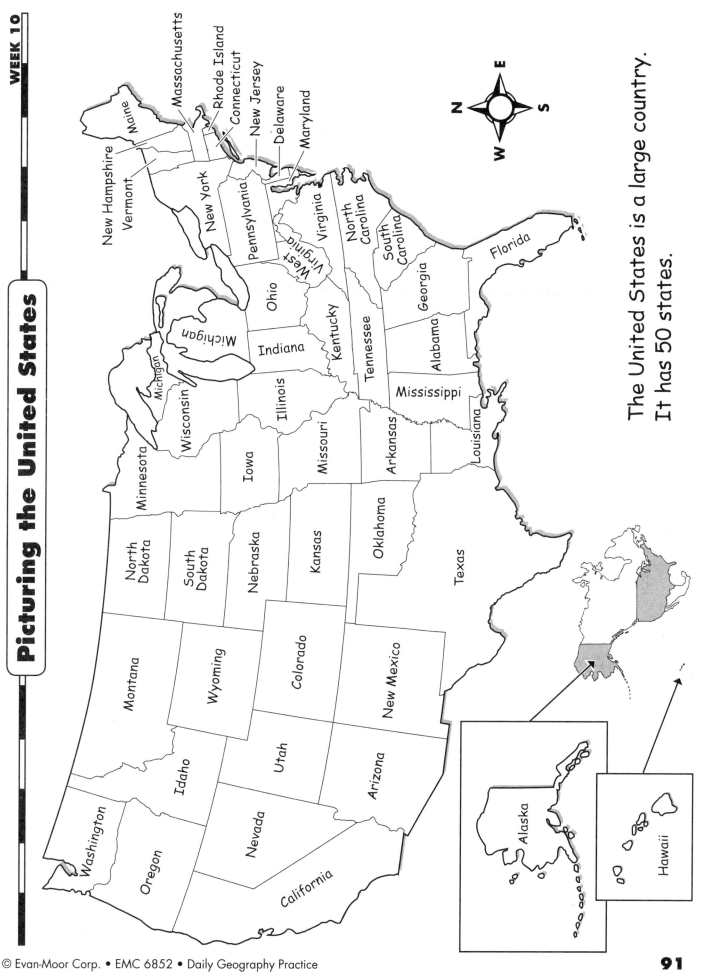

The United States is a large country. It has 50 states.

91

92

A Street Map of Parker

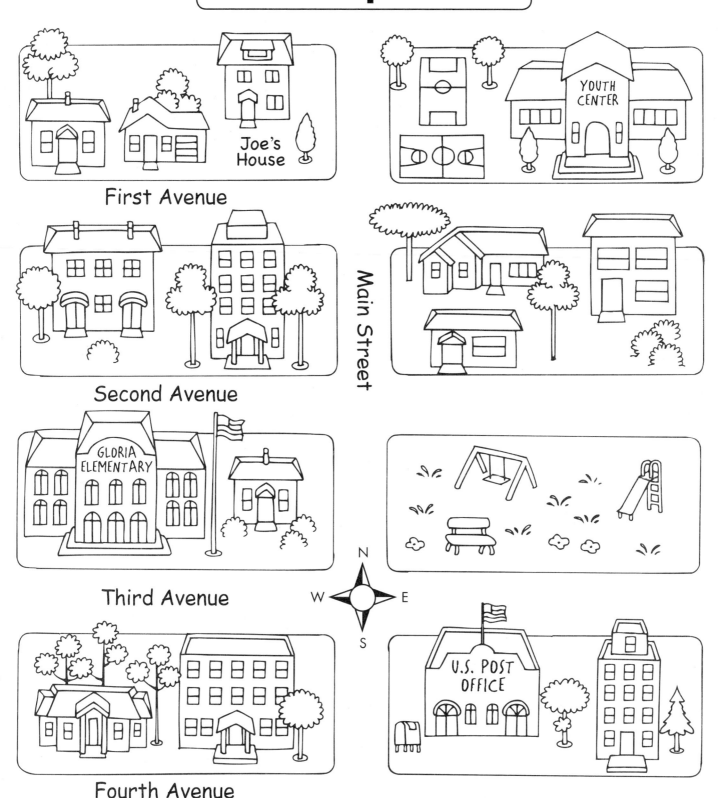

First Avenue

Second Avenue

Main Street

Third Avenue

YOUTH CENTER

GLORIA ELEMENTARY

N
W   E
S

Fourth Avenue

U.S. POST OFFICE

Joe's House

A Road Map of Nebraska

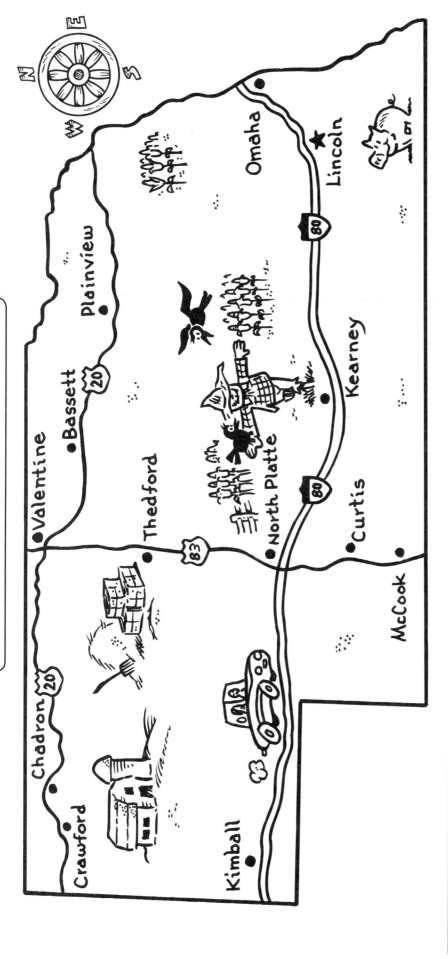

Nebraska is a state. It has lots of roads that cross the state. Three highways are shown on this map. Some cities are shown along the highways.

_____

_____

_____

_____

Map Key

—— 🛡️80 interstate

🛡️20 U.S. highway

★ capital

● city

A World Map

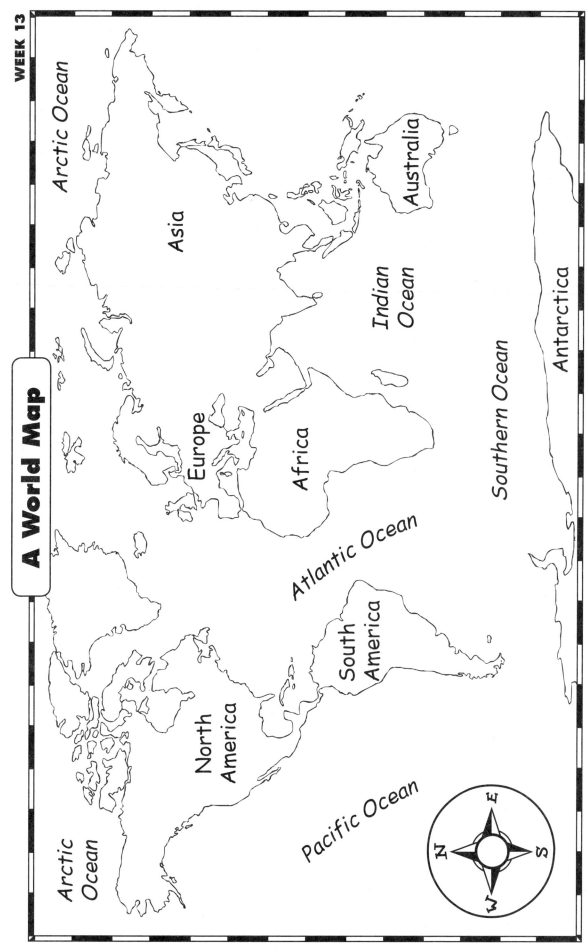

The world has seven large land areas. They are called continents. The world has five large bodies of salt water. They are called oceans.

A Land and Water Map of Washington

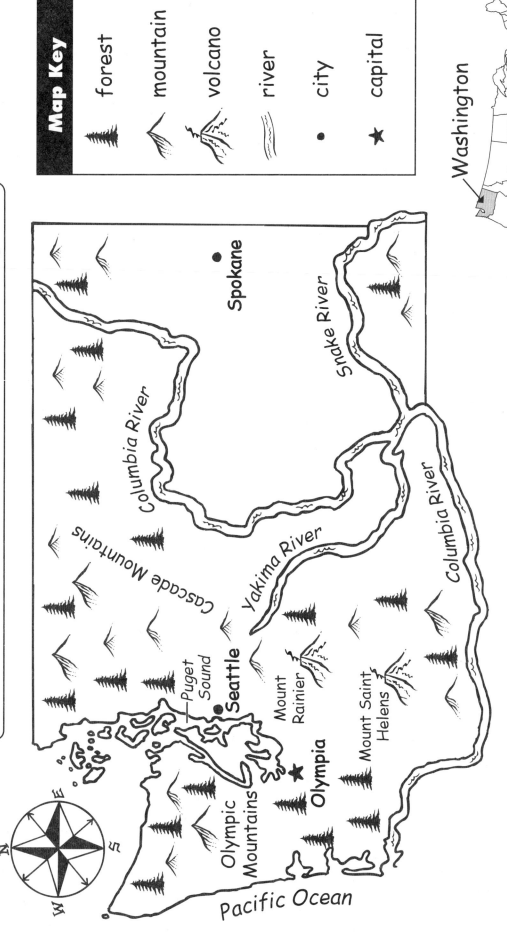

Washington is called "The Evergreen State." It has many forests. Washington also has many mountains. The highest mountain is Mount Rainier. Mount Saint Helens is a famous volcano. Washington borders the Pacific Ocean. Puget Sound is a long body of water. Ships come into Puget Sound.

A Land and Water Map of Arizona

UNITED STATES

Arizona

Arizona has deserts and mountains. It also has the famous Grand Canyon. The Grand Canyon is a deep valley with steep sides. The Colorado River flows through the canyon. The canyon walls are made of layers of rock. The rock layers are in shades of red, yellow, brown, and green.

Map Key

desert	river
mountain	★ capital
canyon	• city

Painted Desert

Grand Canyon

Flagstaff •

Colorado River

Phoenix ★

Gila River

Sonoran Desert

Tucson •

A Land and Water Map of Hawaii

Hawaii is a state in the Pacific Ocean. It is made up of eight main islands.

Map Key

island
volcano
mountain
• city
★ capital

North
East
South
West

Pacific Ocean

KAUAI

NIIHAU

OAHU
Sunset Beach
Pearl Harbor Honolulu
Waikiki Beach

MOLOKAI

LANAI
Maalaea Bay

MAUI
Haleakala Crater

KAHOOLAWE

Pacific Ocean

HAWAII
Hilo
Kilauea Volcano
Kailua-Kona
Mauna Loa Volcano
Hawaii Volcanoes National Park

Island Name Pronunciation

Hawaii (huh WY ee)
Kahoolawe (KAH hoh uh LAH vay)
Kauai (kow WAH ee)
Lanai (lah NAH ee)
Maui (MOW ee)
Molokai (moh loh KAH ee)
Niihau (NEE how)
Oahu (oh AH hoo)

A Land and Water Map of Florida

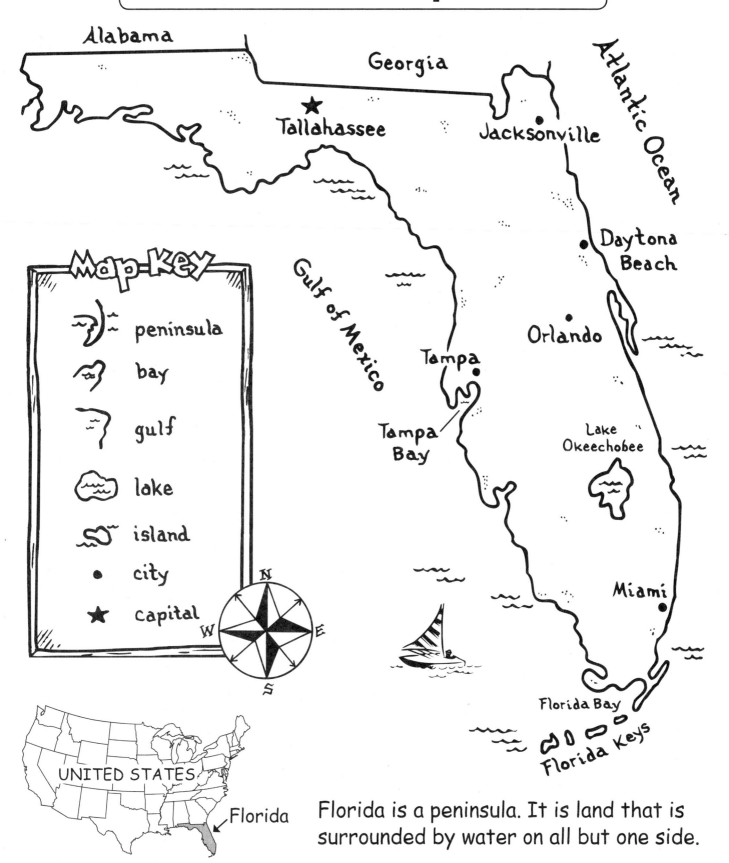

Florida is a peninsula. It is land that is surrounded by water on all but one side.

A Land and Water Map of Minnesota

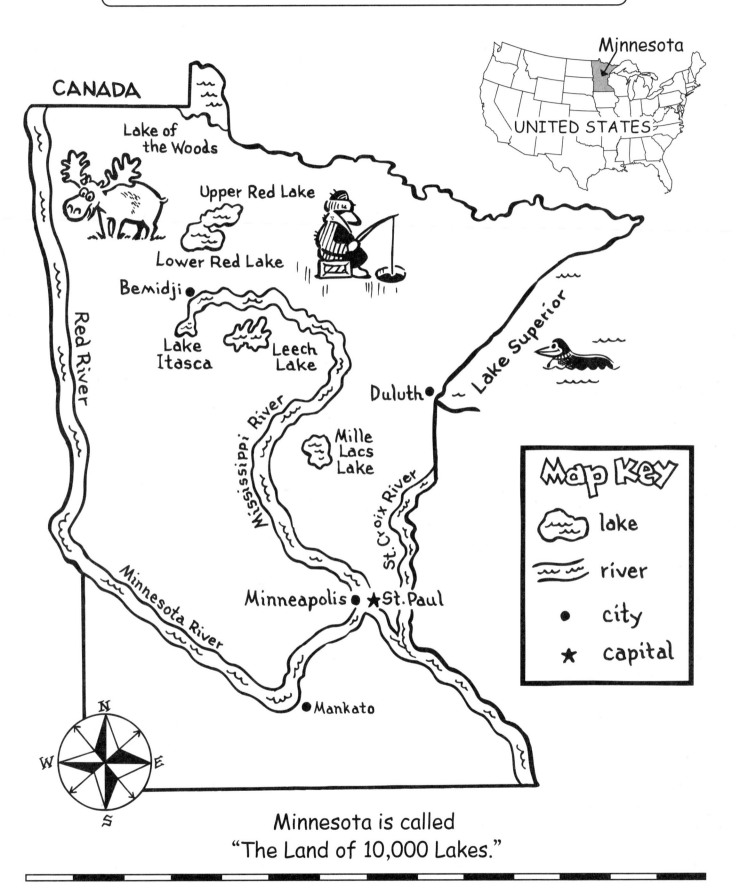

Minnesota is called
"The Land of 10,000 Lakes."

A Rural Area Map

A rural area is in the countryside.
A rural area is a farming community.

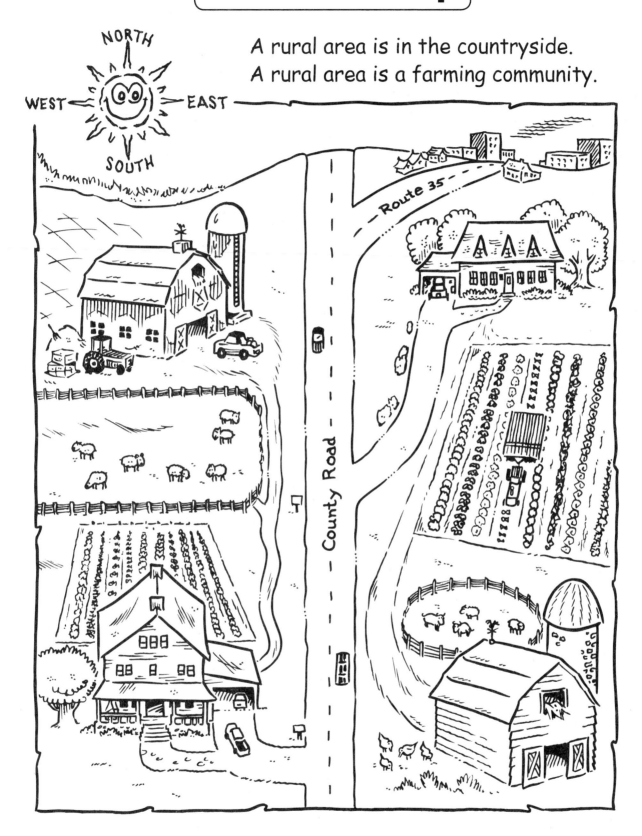

110

A Suburb Map

Fulton Street

Villa Street

Prairie Street

RESTAURANT

PETS

GROCERY

QUICK MART

GAS

Lake Street

Welcome to Elgin

Elgin is a suburb. It is a community near the big city of Chicago.

A City Map of

A city is a busy and crowded place. It has many tall buildings called skyscrapers.

A State Map

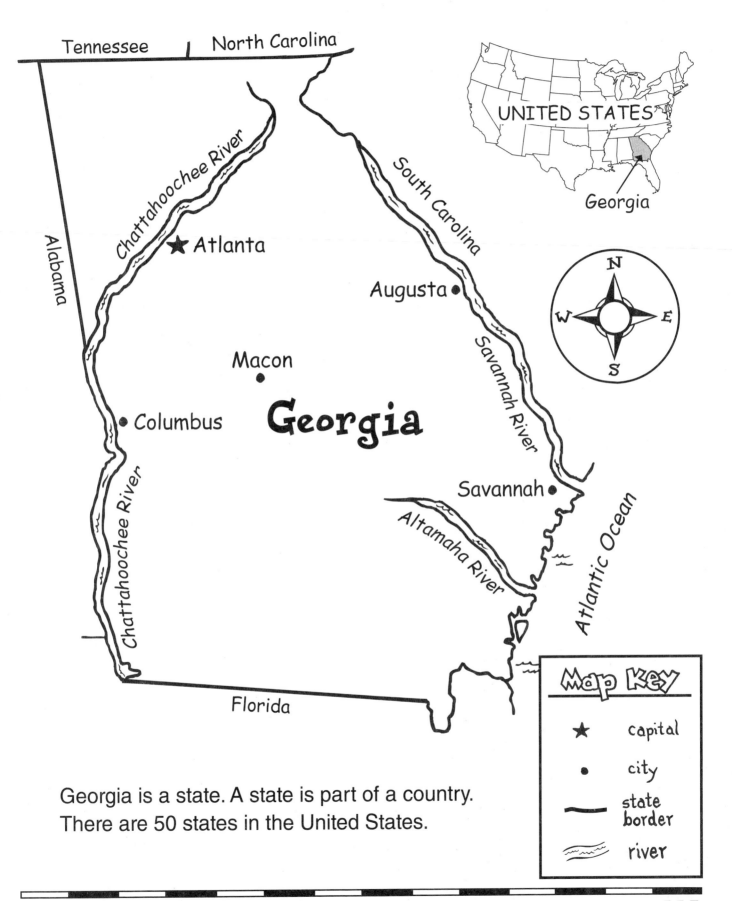

Georgia is a state. A state is part of a country.
There are 50 states in the United States.

An Amusement Park

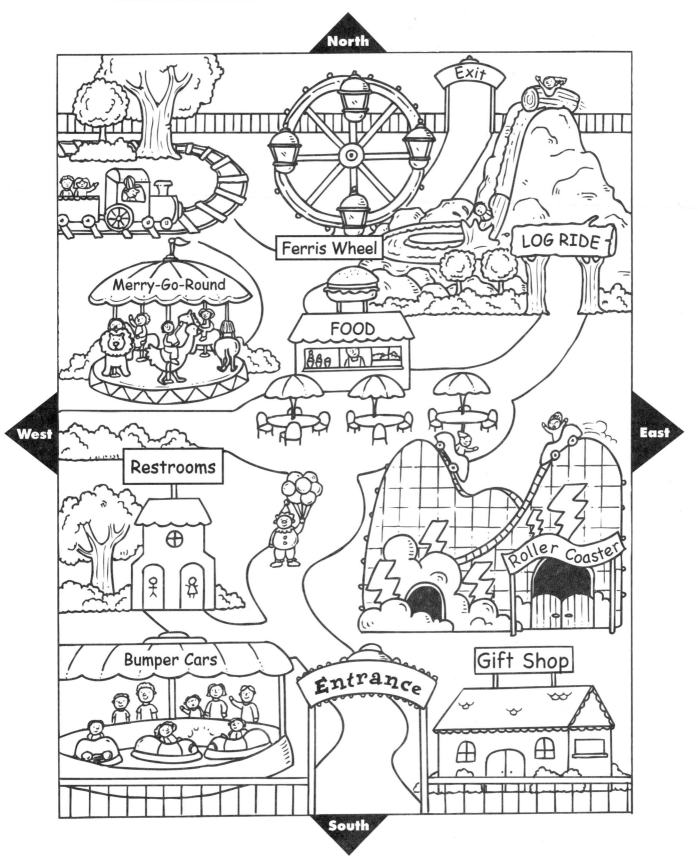

North

Exit

Ferris Wheel

LOG RIDE

Merry-Go-Round

FOOD

West   East

Restrooms

Roller Coaster

Bumper Cars

Gift Shop

Entrance

South

Mount Rushmore

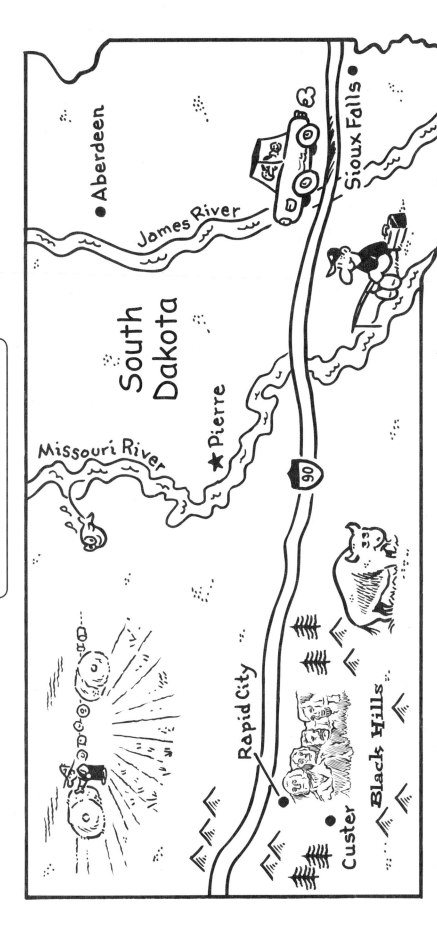

Map Key

⭐ capital   🏔 Mount Rushmore

• city   🌲 forest

🛡 interstate   ⛰ mountain

Aberdeen

James River

Sioux Falls

South Dakota

Missouri River

★ Pierre

90

Rapid City

Custer

Black Hills

Mount Rushmore is a national memorial. It is a large stone carving, or sculpture. It shows the faces of four great presidents.

From left to right, they are George Washington, Thomas Jefferson, Theodore Roosevelt, and Abraham Lincoln.

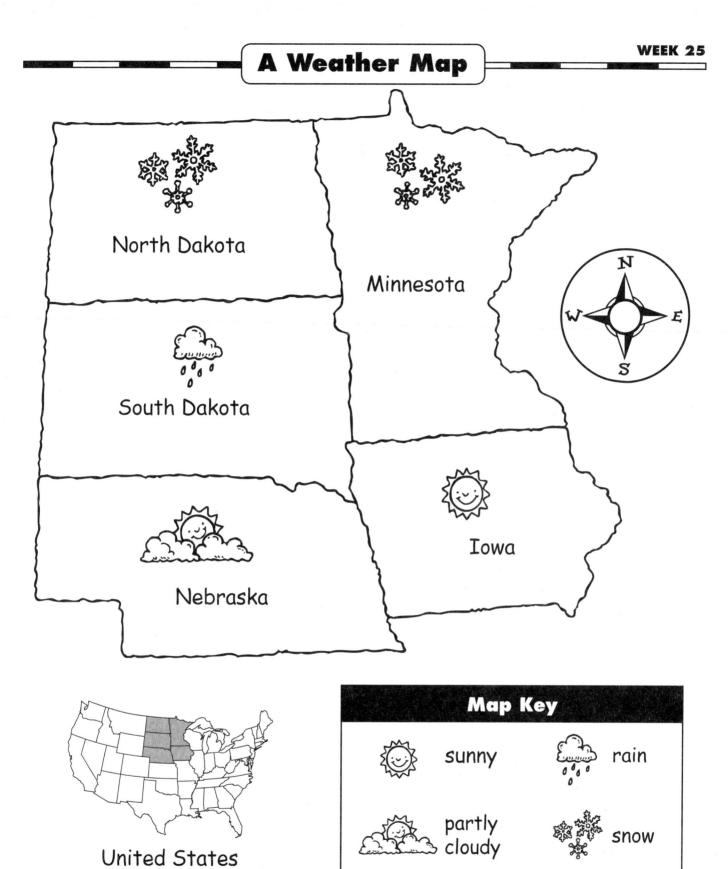

United States

Map Key

☀ sunny   🌧 rain

⛅ partly cloudy   ❄ snow

A Desert Habitat

Desert Animals

coyote
elf owl
lizard
Gila monster
jackrabbit
javelina
kangaroo rat
rattlesnake
roadrunner
scorpion
sidewinder
tarantula

adobe house

prickly pear
cactus

saguaro
cactus

lizard

sidewinder

A desert is a dry place. It gets less than 10 inches of rain each year. People, animals, and plants live in the desert. A desert is their habitat. It is their home.

124

A Population Map of California

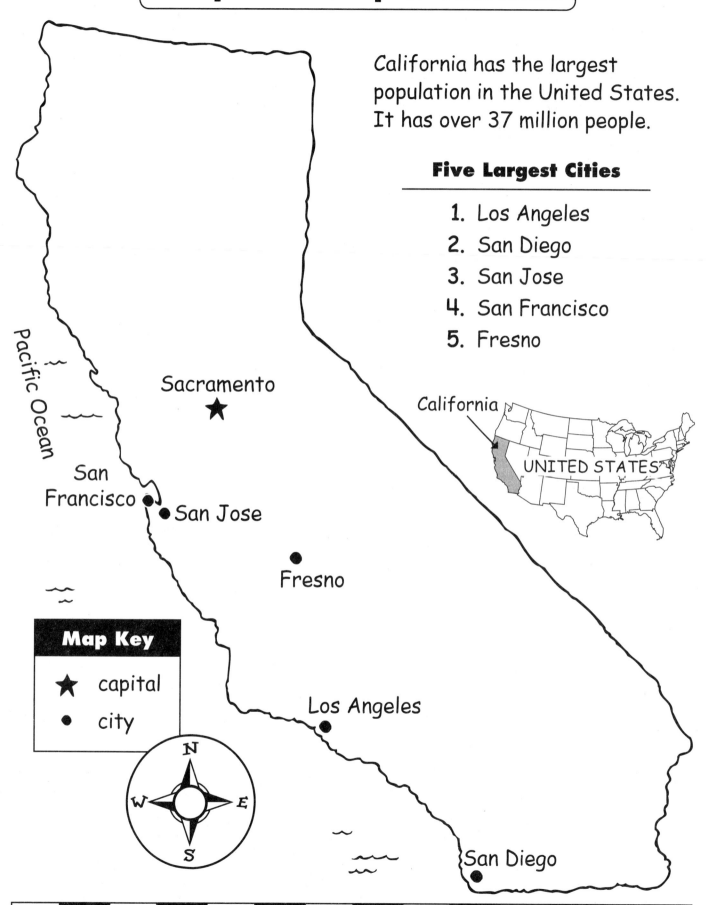

California has the largest population in the United States. It has over 37 million people.

Five Largest Cities

1. Los Angeles
2. San Diego
3. San Jose
4. San Francisco
5. Fresno

California

UNITED STATES

Pacific Ocean

Sacramento

San Francisco

San Jose

Fresno

Map Key

★ capital

● city

N
W E
S

Los Angeles

San Diego

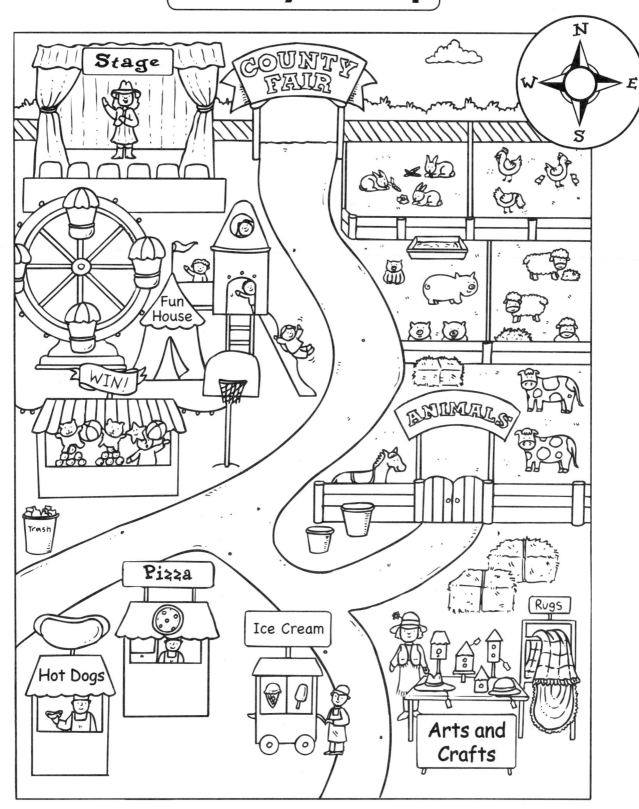

A Product Map of Kansas

Topeka ★

Kansas City •

Wichita •

N E S W (compass)

Map Key

 cattle

 hogs

corn

sorghum

wheat

★ capital

• city

Kansas is called "The Wheat State." It grows more wheat than any other state. Kansas is also called "The Breadbasket of America."

Top Farm Products

1. beef cattle   4. sorghum grain
2. wheat   5. hogs
3. corn

Living in a Community

Roll Avenue

Baker Street

Candy Lane

Cookie Avenue

Draw your house here.

Community Services

Community services are places that help with the needs of the community. They help keep people safe. They help sick people. They help people learn. They help in emergencies.

_____

_____

_____

_____

Cattle Ranches in Texas

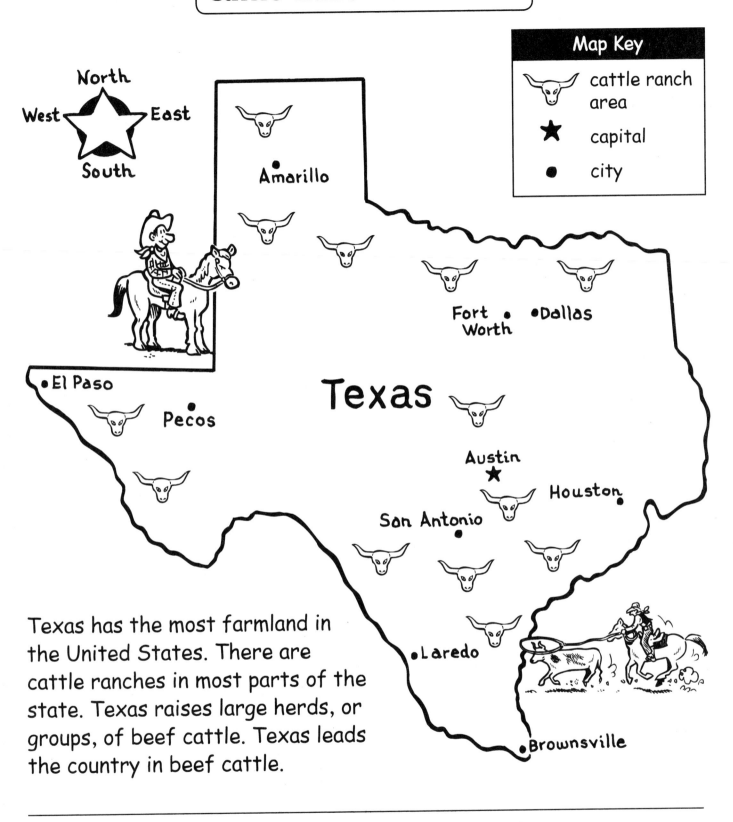

Map Key

🐂 cattle ranch area

★ capital

• city

North
West — East
South

Amarillo

Fort Worth • Dallas

Texas

•El Paso

Pecos

Austin ★

Houston

San Antonio

•Laredo

•Brownsville

Texas has the most farmland in the United States. There are cattle ranches in most parts of the state. Texas raises large herds, or groups, of beef cattle. Texas leads the country in beef cattle.

A Tourist Map of Hawaii

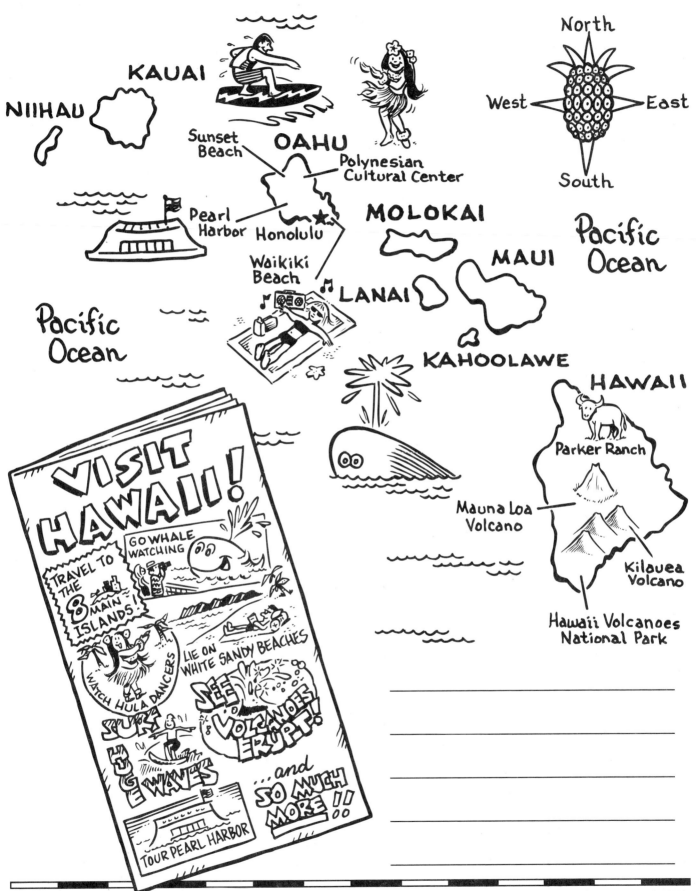

138

A Resource Map of Maine

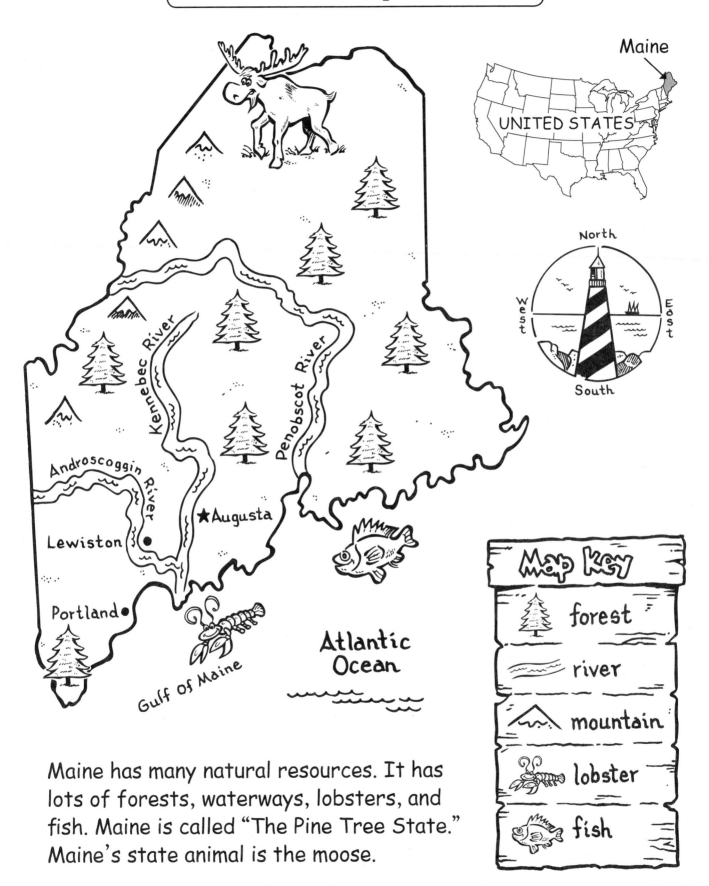

UNITED STATES

Maine

North

West

East

South

Kennebec River

Penobscot River

Androscoggin River

★Augusta

Lewiston

Portland

Gulf of Maine

Atlantic Ocean

Map Key

🌲 forest

〰 river

⌂ mountain

🦞 lobster

🐟 fish

Maine has many natural resources. It has lots of forests, waterways, lobsters, and fish. Maine is called "The Pine Tree State." Maine's state animal is the moose.

Clarksville: Then and Now

Clarksville 150 Years Ago

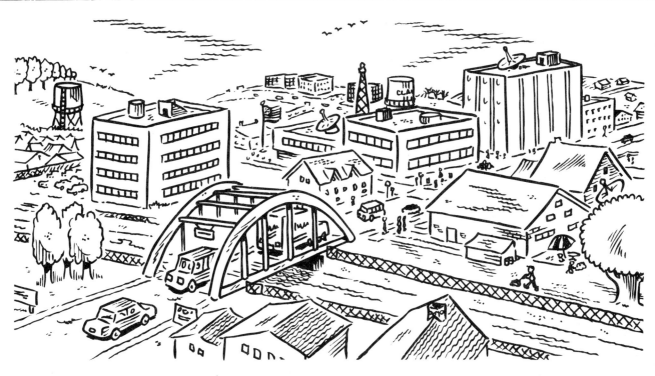

Clarksville Today

_____

_____

_____

A Neighborhood Plan

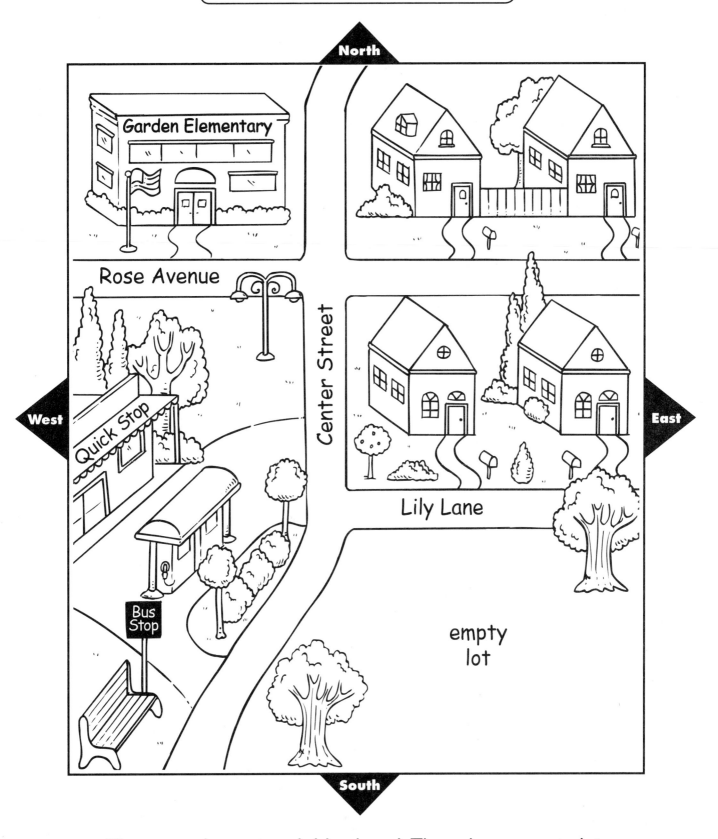

The map shows a neighborhood. There is an empty lot.
What would you build there? Make a plan.

143